The Fundamentals of Capoeira Program

12 Months of Capoeira Martial Arts, Acrobatics, and Capoeira Music

Videos and Guide

Chris Roel

© 2016 by **Chris Roel**

All Rights Reserved.   No part of this publication may be reproduced in any form or by any means, including scanning, photocopying, or otherwise without prior written permission of the copyright holder.

First Printing, 2015

Printed in the United States of America

Liability Disclaimer

By reading this document, you assume all risks associated with using the advice given below, with a full understanding that you, solely, are responsible for anything that may occur as a result of putting this information into action in any way, and regardless of your interpretation of the advice.

You further agree that our company cannot be held responsible in any way for the injury or any temporary discomfort. Please consult with a physician before attempting any program to see if you are fit enough for an exercise regimen.

Terms of Use

You are given a non-transferable, "personal use" license to this product. You cannot distribute it or share it with other individuals.

Also, there are no resale rights or private label rights granted when purchasing this document. In other words, it's for your own personal use only.

The Fundamentals of Capoeira Program

12 Months of Capoeira Martial Arts, Acrobatics, and Capoeira Music

Videos and Guide

Table of Contents

Welcome..9
1 Ginga and Base...............................15
2 Esquivas..21
3 Circular Kicks.................................31
4 Straight Kicks.................................49
5 Movement.......................................59
6 Acrobatics.......................................67
7 Ground Game.................................89
8 Partner Work..................................97
9 Quedas (Takedowns)....................105
10 Music...117
Video System Access Link..............123
About the Author............................125
Other Works by Chris Roel............129

Welcome

Thanks for beginning your journey in the wonderful world of Brazilian Capoeira! This is the art that totally changed my life for the better. You can read all about my transformational journey in my book "Ginga and Grow Strong". For now, forget about me. We want to talk about what Capoeira is going to do for YOU!

The exercise is great, the moves are cool, the music is amazing, and what other place can you learn Brazilian culture, language, dance all while learning self-defense? An old saying in Capoeira is:

Capoeira is like drinking from a fire hydrant. You only take in a little, but you end up all wet.

After my first Capoeira class, I immediately knew what this meant. There seemed like so much to learn, and I was drenched in sweat every class, so don't feel overwhelmed. It's completely natural. We're teaching so many different concepts that it'll take a little longer to master than just kicking and punching. As long as your having fun, it'll make your journey more enjoyable. That being said, don't give up when times get tough. You WILL experience sore muscles, peeling feet, and other growing pains. Everyone hits a plateau. You will persevere through it and achieve your goals. **Make sure to go to the back of the book to get your Video System and Guide access code.** Upon email verification you will gain access to the system. You can do that now and watch the video for each section you read.

Music

The music is very important! Make sure you are clapping and singing in the roda. At first, you won't know many songs but just fake it and make noises with your mouth you feel match the melody. (Ha! Really)

I have included a link in the program to dozens of Capoeira songs our group uses most. Learn these first, or run ahead and learn them all. There are hundreds of Capoeira songs and certain groups only sing certain songs. The songs you sing in my group might not be the ones sang in another group, however, there are some main songs everybody sings like:

>Sim, sim, sim
>Paranauê
>Zum, zum, zum
>and others...

In the first year, in our program, you will be concentrating on clapping, pandeiro, atabaque, agogô bell, and singing the songs. If you get pretty good quickly, I recommend looking into our leadership program. It is for advanced students looking become a Graduado (black belt) in Capoeira. It will include more advanced techniques, music, take downs, historical knowledge, grappling, and character development. But don't worry about that now. You should concentrate on the following.

Fundamentals

If you train outside of your regular class, you will get better. Although you can train a variety of things like aerial acrobatics, grappling, and more, I recommend that you stick to the fundamentals. Ginga, esquivas, basic circular kicks, base, and learning the Capoeira songs. The sooner you can move like a Capoeirista in the most fundamental form, the better your development will be moving into the intermediate level.

Brazilian Portuguese

You will learn an immense amount of Portuguese without even knowing it! Through the music sang in the roda, this constant reinforcement will sneak in your Portuguese lesson in a fun way. If you feel the need, buy a basic conversational or grammatical Portuguese book at your local bookstore.

Once I fell in love with the music, I needed more so I ran and bought a couple to turbo charge my Brazilian Portuguese. In the first year, make sure to have fun. You will be working hard just getting in shape doing the basic movements, so make sure you don't burn out. If you feel really motivated to excel, then go ahead.

That being said, let's get ready embark on an amazing journey! "Vamo' Gingar!"

Chapter 1
Ginga and Base

The Ginga is the most important and fundamental movement in Brazilian Capoeira. The swinging of the body has three basic positions: Ginga left, base, and Ginga right. The base, also called cadeira in other groups, is the parallel foot position with wide stance and hands up protecting. There are several variations, but let's just consider version for Ginga.

The Ginga left position describes the position at the far left of the Ginga. Right leg is back deep, the right elbow is up protecting the face, the left arm is elevated for balance, and the knees are bent keeping a strong low center of gravity.

The Ginga right position is exactly opposite the Ginga left position. It describes the the position furthest right of the Ginga. Left leg is back, left elbow is up protecting the face, right arm is elevated for balance, and knees are bent keeping a strong low center of gravity.

Although we learn this three separate positions, the Ginga is performed seamlessly at the tempo of whatever Capoeira music is playing. The toque (rhythm) of the berimbau (bowed stick instrument) commands the tempo of the martial arts game. If the rhythm is slow, the game is funky and playful. If the music is fast, then it is more of a combat game. Listen to the music, but also listen to your instructor. He/she may have a specific modification on your training that day, like no sweeps, kicks only, only a certain acrobatic, etc.

Ginga Left

Base/Cadeira

Ginga Right

Matching Up the Ginga
When Gingaing with a partner there are two different variations: Regular and Cross Ginga. For the purpose of the Fundamental Program, we will only concentrate on the Regular Ginga orientation.

For the Regular Ginga orientation with your partner, you will be exactly mirrored. While facing your partner in Ginga left position, your partner will be in Ginga right position. You bother will transition through base at the same time into opposite Ginga positions respectively. This is the basis of all attacks, escapes, acrobatics, and flourishes. Always practice the Ginga. It will strengthen your quads, hamstrings, calves, back, and more. As you get stronger and more comfortable, try to drop your base more and more, always with a straight back. This is to resist take downs, strengthen your own take downs, and be less of a target. Standing straight up makes you really easy to hit.

Chapter 2
Esquivas

The Capoeira style is one of dodging and counterattacking. Instead of hard blocks like you would see in traditional martial arts, we would rather not be there for the blow. This gives Capoeira its smooth aesthetic, and also works the core immensely. The fundamental student will learn to moves his/her torso up, down, and side to side all while keeping a solid base on the floor.

In the Fundamental program we will talk about four main dodges: Cocorinha, Esquiva (frontal), Esquiva Lateral, and Quebrada. Don't worry if you have a buddy who trains Capoeira and calls the same moves by different names. Remember that Capoeira was developed in secret by different Capoeira masters. It was spread from master to disciple independently and carried down the names what each particular master called them. Just know what we call them, and how to perform them.

Cocorinha

This dodge is the easiest, and the one we teach kids who don't have a lot of leg coordination yet. Don't be misled, though, this is a very disarming dodge. What looks like a harmless squat, a Capoeira player can counter dangerously from this position.

The Cocorinha dodge is performed by squatting all the way down with both feet solidly on the floor, bottom down, and with one elbow up blocking over head. Your other hand can touch the ground for more balance. Many students dodge with elbow only protecting their mouth level. Don't do this.

It only takes one kick to the head for you to learn to listen to your instructor, so hold you elbow up right over your head blocking. Although it's a dodge, you want to be wary of low kicks and attacks. Better safe than sorry.
There is Cocorinha left and right positions by switching your protecting hand. The left is at the furthest left position of the Ginga and vice versa.

Esquiva (frontal)

This is the dodge we usually teach first to adults and most able bodied kids. It involves a big lunge with the knee not touching floor, opposite hand flat on the ground for balance, head tilted slightly to keep an eye on the attacker, and the other elbow up blocking at head level. Once again there is Esquiva left and right positions described by which side of the Ginga it is performed at.

If you are at the left side of the Ginga, then your right leg will be all the way back, straight and solid, while your left leg is bent, your left palm on the ground, etc.

Esquiva Lateral

This is performed by arriving in the middle of the Ginga in base and leaning the torso over to one side, either left or right. The inside elbow is up protecting at head level, while the head is tilted keeping an eye on the attacker. The other hand can be out to the side elevated, or bent under the torso ready to counterattack. Once again there is left and right positions of this dodge.

Quebrada

In the Quebrada dodge you are turned perpendicular to your partner. The front elbow is up protecting the head, the back arm is elevated for balance, and the head is tilted to keep a low profile. The back is straight like a board and knees are bent with a wide stance. When using this dodge, you want to face away from an attack, so that the struck your back would take the brunt of the force--not your front.

As mentioned earlier there's right and left position dodge. These four dodges should be practiced with Ginga five times each side for kids, and 10 times each side for adults. We include the last three in our warm-up every single fundamental class.

You must train your core, torso, legs and back in this fashion. You will get strong, coordinated, and nimble with these movements alone. Now we will introduce you to the kicks.

Chapter 3
Circular Kicks

Capoeira has it's certain style, like all martial arts. The fundamental circular kicks in Capoeira are characterized by not being chambered. This means that they are performed with a lock leg and no knee snapping the calf and foot either way. Although we have those kicks, too, they are are not characteristic of the Capoeira style.

First we'll talk about the inside swinging kick known as Passa Pé.

Passa Pé
In other groups this kick is known as Meia Lua de Frente. I'll explain it starting from a Ginga right position. From Ginga right, you step to the base with the left foot. Instead of stepping back with the left foot, you lift your leg and swing it in semi-circle from your right to left attacking at about waist level for now. At the furthest left position of this attack, the leg bends and returns to the floor at the base (parallel) position and sends you back to the Ginga with left leg going back into Ginga right

position. There are other variations, but this is the most fundamental. To perform Passa Pé left, just follow the above instructions with opposite legs and positioning.

The hands should be maintained up and protecting while performing this attack. We will now discuss the three remaining fundamental circular kicks. These are back kicks, meaning they hit with the outside of the foot, while the Passa Pé was striking with the inside of the foot going forwards from the Ginga.

Quexada

This is the most fundamental of the three circular back kicks. Make sure to learn this one first, at least decently, before moving on.

You first initiate the movement by turning into the Quebrada dodge. Then, while perpendicular to your opponent, your back foot will step behind your front foot to charge your hips like winding up a rubber band. You will then release your kick with the front foot making a semi-circle back kick, finishing all the way in the back (Ginga position right/left). Remember that these are not chambered kicks. The leg should be locked straight as a board with toes flexed back towards your face, and heel exposed.

Once you get the feel of it, you will use your Ginga and upper body to swing your kick as it cuts through the air. You will be using little kick energy, only to chop your leg down with conviction, but never bending it until it hits the ground in the back.

Armada

This is essentially a Quexada with a spin before it. Let's talk about the details. From the Ginga right position you will step to the base with the left leg, then immediately step with the right leg diagonally right in-front of your left shoulder. Once your right foot is planted solidly on the floor with good base, you will begin to rotate your torso counter-clockwise (left) with your hands up. Do not step any more, just keep rotating and pivoting until your head and torso can see your target. (Use a mirror and once you see yourself you are where you need to be) Then you are ready to release your back kick in the same fashion described in Quexada. Your hips are charged so just lift your front leg (left) and kick in a semi-circle, keeping it locked with toes flexed back until the leg lands solidly to the back. Remember to land in Ginga left position with your right position with your left hand protecting.

To perform the Armada right, just do the opposite of the instructions described above. These circular kicks are very important in Capoeira. You'll do hundreds, and over time thousands. For now, just try to do 25 left and 25 right. The next kicks is probably the hardest of the three fundamental circular kicks.

Meia Lua de Compasso
This is the Capoeira kick. A reverse wheel heel kick. If you look up "20-second MMA Capoeira knockout" on Youtube, this is the kick the fighter uses. This is a brutal, beautiful kick if done right, so be careful with your training partner. It takes a long time develop a good straight one, so don't get discouraged and keep practicing. I usually break down this kick into three positions, but let's start from the Ginga right position.

Step to the base strongly with the left foot. Then with your right foot step across your opposite shoulder like in the previous kick, only this time take a deeper step and lean on your right leg having it support about 75% of your weight. Your head will be upside down under your crotch, while your left leg is elongated and straight. This is position one of MLC.

In step two of MLC your left leg releases from the back to kick a semi-circle leading with the heel. Let's stop and do a progress check. Your left leg should be outstretched facing your target locked and toes flexed back towards your body. You should have two hands flat on the floor as your pivoting mechanism, with head upside down looking at your target from below your crotch.

Position three is the finishing position. Continue the movement of the semi-circular kick landing to the back in Ginga right position. Remember not to bend the leg until it hits home in the back. It'll take some practice to keep it straight throughout the move, but that's what makes this such a beautiful kick. You can start with 25 each side of this kick to practice, but once you get used to it, aim for 50 each side. You're going to need to do a lot of these kicks to get a decent one.

Chapter 4
Straight Kicks

These are the kicks that you can find in probably all other martial arts. They are fundamental in attacking with the legs. For the fundament program, we will concentrate on just three, but learn to use them out of the Ginga. The Ginga is a nice way to disguise these kicks, and a great way to add momentum and power to any attack. Let's begin.

Bençāo
This is the front push kick. Starting from Ginga right position, step to the base once again with your left foot. Then, your right knee comes to right about chest level (depending on target) and extends to straighten your leg in a front attack. You will be kicking with the bottom of your foot with hips out. After the kick, bring the leg back in then to base then stepping back to Ginga right position with your left leg. When performing this kick, envision kicking down a door.

Ponta Pé (Cruzado)

This is the Capoeira version of a roundhouse kick. Most other groups call this a Martelo. Starting from the Ginga right position, step to the base with your left foot, then lift the right knee. From here you will pivot on your left foot turning your hips sideways to the left. From here your right bent leg should look like a table top. You should be able to put a ball on it without it falling. The leg then extends to kick (chambers) striking your with the top of your foot, not the toes. You then retract your foot back to table top position, rotate your hips back straight, and set down your right foot on the floor either at the base or to the back as you return to Ginga.

As mentioned earlier, do the opposite side steps to perform the left Ponta Pé.

Pisão

This is a Capoeira side kick. Although we will be learning different variations of the side kick, or Pisão, for the Fundamental program we're going to learn it using the Ginga to maximize momentum and to use Capoeira movement dynamics. First, while Gingaing we will stop in Ginga right position, turn into Quebrada right position, then begin the movement. Our back (left leg) steps behind our front leg towards our target, only this time we point our left heel at our target like the crosshairs of a gun. From this position, our right knee comes up to our chest, then out sideways to strike our target with the bottom of our foot. The kick retracts back into the chest, then we pivot on the left foot, rotating hips to the right to set our foot to the back in Ginga left position.

To perform the other side, just use opposite directions. Remember to concentrate on these three main straight kicks. In the future, when learning more advanced versions, you will need a solid foundation with good fundamental ability.

Chapter 5
Movement

We're going to focus on two main fundamental movements. It is important to know what these are and how to perform them. It is how a Capoeira player moves around. Also, we will build on these when doing combinations, escapes, and acrobatics.

Rolé

The Rolé is a forward oriented Capoeira spin, or roll (not really). Starting from Base with hands up protecting from any attack, lean to left touching the ground with two hands and let your head naturally go upside down, making sure to keep eye contact with your opponent. This will make your right leg light, so swing it across towards the left until you end up in a wide legged stance, bottom facing your opponent, two hands flat on the ground, and with your head looking at your opponent upside down. Basically, you will be bent over. This is just a transitional position, don't worry. Then to complete the movement, continue rotating in the same direction by taking your left leg and swinging it to base. This will make your body come right side up facing your opponent with hands up protecting. We use the Rolé very frequently, and it's a very niece way to get around in the roda.

You can do this to the other direction as well. Just use opposite directions.

Escapa

Some groups call this Giro de Costa. This, essentially, is a Rolé in reverse. There are different set ups and many different variations. The one I'm about to describe is the very basic one we that we ask for when testing our students for their second cord (belt).

It starts out faking a MLC kick. Starting from Ginga right position, step to the base with the left foot, then take that deep Meia Lua de Compasso step with the right foot while touching the floor with both hands and head upside down. Now instead of kicking the right foot in the air, the left foot drags on the floor until its parallel with the right foot. Make sure you have a wide stance and maintain both hands on the floor and keep looking upside down. This will help you keep your balance and keep an eye on your opponent. Your head then follows around to the direction of your left foot and leading with your hands protecting ends up in Base position. The word "Escapa" means escape. You'll see how we use it to escape an attack and pop up behind our opponent, or just use it as a cool dynamic movement in itself.

Chapter 6
Acrobatics

This is the amazing part of this martial art. When most people think of Capoeira, they think of the cool moves. It's what makes it different than just kicking and punching. It's not just gymnastics or cheer acrobatics, it has its own Brazilian swing and style. In the fundamental program we will just go over the basics. But don't worry. Your socks will be blown off. Cartwheels, monkey flips, hand spins, bridges, Capoeira aerials, etc. are just a few. Let's get started with the basics.

Aú

This is the Capoeira cartwheel. There are some major differences between an Aú and a regular gymnastics cartwheel. First, its starts off in the base position with wide stance and hands in front protecting. We don't want to hold our hands up in the air like a gymnast and put one foot forward because that's just begging to be kicked in the ribs or stomach. Remember, this is a martial art so we want to be protected, even when initiating an acrobatic movement.

It starts off from the base, but let's go ahead and start it from Ginga right position to gain momentum to throw us into the movement. From the Ginga right position, step to the base with the left foot solidly on the ground and hands up in front protecting. From there reach to the floor on the left with both hands like performing a Rolé. Instead of sweeping the right leg forward, it goes up in the air and goes over the top as you put all your weight on your hands. The left leg follows in the air, then the right leg lands first on the other side of your body next to the right hand, and then the left foot lands putting your in base position with hands up protecting.

You'll need to develop upper body and core strength to get your legs going directly over the top. Don't worry you'll still be able to perform the move at the beginner level, just pass your feet out in front of your body instead of over the top. Repeat with opposite directions to perform the right Aú.

Macaco

This is the monkey flip, a very nice backwards flipping motion. Don't worry we'll build you up like the last move. For this acrobatic we're going to start in a Cocorinha right position, only instead of facing towards our opponent, we will be facing perpendicular (to the right). Then we will switch our hands. Left hand on the floor behind us fingers facing away and with palm flat on the ground. Our right hand will be straight up in the air. We will stretch three times, each time lifting our hips off the ground as if to do a high bridge. On the the third stretch, we will jump from our Cocorinha position to touch the floor with our outstretched hand to touch the floor, then our right leg will follow, and finally our left leg. It will resemble a backwards facing cartwheel, but once you get good at it, you will be going over the top and making it look more like a dirty back handspring.

Repeat with opposite directions to do a right Macaco.

Ponte

This is the Capoeira bridge. Like an acrobatics or dance bridge it involves laying down on your back, putting your hands, elbows towards the ceiling, by your ears palm down on the floor. You fingers should be facing your feet, and your feet should be on the floor close to your bottom. That means to bend your knees all the way. Using the floor you will push off with all appendages until you rise off the ground.

Try to get your belly button as high as possible and stretch until your arms and legs are fully extended. If you need a spot, have a buddy help you get off the floor with a hand, or hands, on your back pushing your upwards as much as you need. First try to do ten bridge push ups. Then once you get stronger, 15, and then finally 20.

When you can perform 20 high bridge push ups by yourself with no spot, you are ready for the the Ponte rotation.

Ponte Rotation

The Ponte, or bridge, rotation begins on all fours facing down. Your palms are flat on the floor and your bottom is up in the air. You then step with the right foot backwards over your left foot rotating causing your right hand to come off the ground and your belly button to start facing the the ceiling. Make sure you have a solid base on the ground, legs evenly separated. As you continue to rotate, make sure you use your legs pushing off the ground lo lift your hips as high as possible. Then look up at your right hand as it passes over your head and lands on the floor slowly and stops in the bridge position--two palms on the floor.

To get out of this position, shift your weight to and lock your right arm. Pick up you left hand as you roll "out of bed" to the right where finally your left leg rotates over your right leg and you finish in a base position. This one takes some practice, but make sure you put in the time. This simple acrobatic is just the beginning for more advanced moves. You will need the back flexibility provided by this exercise to keep progressing to more amazing things. Make sure you build up to the level to rotate both directions. Good luck.

Aú Sem Mão
This is essentially an Aú with no hands, or a Capoeira aerial. I was very impressed when I started training Capoeira with how my instructor broke down each move I believed to be complicated into easy steps where over a few seconds, I was doing a simple variation. Then over a few weeks, I

was doing the move solidly, and over few months I was doing an advanced variation. You, too will learn these awesome moves in this fashion.

First, start in the Base position with hands up in front protecting. Like a skateboard on a half-pipe, your head and torso is going to dip down by your right knee, follow a path under your waistline, all the way up on the left leg. As your head, torso and arms come up on the left side of your body your right leg will kick up in the air as if to jump over a little imaginary fence that would be positioned to your left.
At the same time through your hands up like Superman to further drive the momentum (set). Your right foot should land first and then your left ending in the Base position. Learning this move like this first will have you doing the move right away. Over time your head will go lower and your feet will go higher in the air, making it a legitimate Cartwheel with no hands. Right now it will resemble what's called a butterfly kick. No biggie. It's still awesome, and you're still awesome.

Reverse the moves to do the other side. Also, once you get the basic steps, use the Ginga to throw some extra momentum into the movement. That means start from Ginga right position and do the instructions as described.

Amazonas

This is THE Capoeira move. When people think of Capoeira tricks, this is the one. Also, people think this is a breakdancing move, so you have to add the kick to make it look Capoeira style. We'll worry about that later. I'm talking about the one handed handstand kick we call Amazonas.

We'll first start by using a partner to spot us. As your partner grabs your left hand while standing in front of you reach with your right hand to floor. Your right hand should be flat palmed and placed immediately to the outside of your right foot. You don't want to travel too much to the side. As all your weight goes onto your right hand bring both your feet in the air (left then right) into a hand stand. Do ten left and then ten right.

At this strength and balance stage, we just want to be able to do a handstand. Once you have the basic idea,then have your partner hold your left hand with with his right hand and turn slightly away. Then do the same movement, but this time add a kick (left foot) hitting your partner in the back of the arm or back. Be careful not to kick the spine. You will have to deliver the kick and then return your foot back to landing position. Do this ten times each side as well.

Once you got the idea, try a few (5) on your own with no spot. Once again, first try with no kick, and then add the kick. Over time you WILL get this amazing move. Some students see faster progress if they have dance or acrobatic experience, but it took me a while. After training it for like a week, I started seeing results, but remember, I was a chubby hubby.

Your results may vary. I was an out of shape dad, so just keep trying. You'll get it.

Pião de Mão

This is amazing! The hand spin, although sounds complicated, with the way our program teaches it in a step by step format, You WILL get it, too! I am a believer. I never though I would be doing the moves I am today. Let's get spinning.

1. In the first step of this movement, you will raise your right hand over head and touch your left foot bending in half at the

waist. Don't squat, we need the momentum from this diagonal movement to throw us into the ground acrobatic. Keep doing this back and forth until you got it.

2. In step two, remove your left leg back wards just as soon as your about to touch it with your hand. This may cause you to lose balance. That's okay. Your right hand should invert and touch the ground palm down fingers towards you. Once again, do this several times until you get it. Your hand should be right where your foot was, not anywhere else.

3. Step three is a repetition of steps one and two, but this time you will go into a handstand facing the opposite direction one hand at a time. Fight the urge to put two hands down at once. That will stop you from spinning. Set your right hand down, and then your left going across your body. You will feel the movement start to spin you.

4. In step four, just wait a little longer to put the the second hand on the floor. This will really start to make you spin. Just get your feet all the way up in the air and together. Many students have trou-

ble with this part, so don't worry. Just keep trying and you'll get it. In the basic version your left leg will land first.
Good luck! It's an awesome move.

Martelo Rodado

This a jumping spinning round house kick. Yeah...it's cool. Make sure you know armada first before attempting this kick. Starting from the Ginga right position step to the base with the left foot, then right left across your shoulder as if initiating an armada. Rotate the torso, look over your shoulder, but instead of kicking your long locked leg, you will bring your left knee up to your chest. At this point in time you will be standing on one leg (right) and one knee (left) tucked into your chest with hands up protecting.

From here you will jump and switch legs while rotating your hips to the left. Your left leg lands and your right leg kicks the Ponta Pé before continuing with the momentum and spinning to the left. Don't stop on a dime. Keep the momentum and let the movement die out naturally by spinning again to the left back to Base. Repeat this steps for the other leg.

Once you got the basic steps, use the Ginga to really add some momentum and jump higher and make it a really spectacular kick.

Bananeira
This is just a handstand, but we will tell you the three basic variations we do in the fundamental program. There are many advanced variations, but we'll start here. We need to build strength in the arms and shoulders as well as balance in the body.

<u>Regular</u>-up against the wall first, you will have legs together aligned straight with the shoulders. Hold for 20 second intervals
<u>Splits</u>-same as before only now open your legs as wide as possible. Do 20 second intervals as well.
<u>Split claps</u>-you will alternate from the first and second positions 20 times as if clapping you ankles together. This will develop a lot of body control and upper body

strength. Once you can master these on the wall, try them away from the wall.

Along with this regimen, try walking forwards and backwards on your hands the distance of 50 feet. You need to be agile in Capoeira, whether on your feet or on your hands. You don't have to start that way, but you will become that way.

Chapter 7
Ground Game

Capoeira is truly amazing. Along with the cool aerial acrobatic, martial arts, and music, there's what's called ground movements, or ground game. Once you've got the basics check out my Ground Game System here http://bit.ly/oreisystem. It'll take your ground game to the Intermediate level. For now, let's learn the fundamentals.

Queda de Rins (balled up)

An actual translation of this phrase means, "falling on the kidneys". Sounds appealing right? Ha! Well, it's not as seems. The QDR as we'll abbreviate it is like a yoga or beak dancing elbow stall. It starts as follows.

Start from a squatted position, bottom all the way down, knees all the way bent. Lean to the right side putting your flat right palm on the floor, head, and right palm on the floor around the floor in front of you neck. Your right elbow will be straight up into your ribs or hip acting as a stool to balance on. Play with the positioning but you should have a tripod of appendages helping you balance as you bring your knees into your chest to simulate a ball. Stay with it, it takes some playing with. Don't worry 80 year old yoga grandmas do this move, so you can too. Repeat on the other side.

QDR (Legs staggered)

There's three main QDR positions in the fundamental program, however, there are probably endless variations. We will include two additional QDR positions that will get you prepped to start doing intermediate movements also.

The legs staggered means that your perform the QDR as described previously, and instead of balling up your legs, you either have your top leg forward/bottom leg back or vice versa. You should perform and practice these positions 10 times each side to gain strength, body control, and balance.

Meia Lua Encaixada (push-ups)

This move is awesome because it prepares you for a very nice ground movement that makes you look like your floating on the floor. It starts from a left MLC (Meia Lua de Compasso) position one entrance. Instead of slinging the kick, you enter into QDR in the following manner. Your left leg lifts as if kicking MLC, but you immediately fall on your right elbow and look back left keeping your legs in a V-shape. You then push back where you came returning your leg in a parallel position but your hands remain on the floor. Go up and down like push ups 10 each side. This will strengthen you core, arms, and balance for doing the real MLC encaixada.

Negativa de Angola (push ups)

This is simulating a negativa we have by the same name. Start with your right leg extended and your left leg bent all the way. You will be on the floor with your left foot elevated on the ball. Your right leg will be supported by the outside of the right foot toes pointed to the right. You will have just your right palm on the floor with your other hand either up in the air or out flared to the left. You will initiate a push-up touching your right elbow to your ribs, going up and down. If you need help, then just use both hands, but make sure to make it a goal to start doing one handers as soon as possible. Do 10 each side then build up to at least 15 each side.

Chapter 8
Partner Work

You guys have come a long way. Make sure you understand the basics of your spinning kicks and straight kicks before attempting partner work with those particular techniques used. Capoeira is awesome but now your will begin to understand why the dance is so important. Any martial has kick, punch, elbow, block, etc. Now that you know the Capoeira kicks and dodges, the timing and movement play such a bigger role. Make sure you can Ginga synched up with your partner before doing any of the following exercises.

We will first learn to dodge each kick, then learn to counter, then do some very cool weaving exercises. Let's begin. Vamos embora!

Dodging Partner Work
Have your partner Ginga with you mirroring your steps. He/she will perform a Quexada and you will dodge correctly using Esquiva, 5 times each side. Quexada, although the simplest of the three spinning

kicks is the trickiest to read because it's a half spinning kick that usually whips back across your Ginga. The other two spinning kicks are bigger and easier to read. After doing 5 each side, move on to using Esquiva Lateral, and finally Quebrada.

Go through all the kicks in this fashion using the three different dodges. Go ahead and switch with your partner as well. You give the kicks and he/she dodges. Here are some basic tips on how to dodge correctly.

When using Esquiva, you want to block with your inside hand where the attack is coming from. Your outside hand will be supporting your weight on the floor. As mentioned earlier the Quexada is tricky, so make sure your hands and legs are coordinated correctly as described in the Dodge section of this book. Also remember to be on the correct side of the Ginga. If your on Ginga left position you will Esquiva with left hand touching the floor and right hand blocking.

When using Esquiva lateral, lean away from the kick and use your inside elbow for blocking as described in the paragraph before. Don't look at the ground as sometimes we get scared of the attack. Make sure to tilt your head toward the attack to see your opponent. If you're blocking correctly you won't be in any danger. Also, as you become more and more flexible, you will be able to dodge closer and lower. That's a good thing.

When using Quebrada, turn your back to the kick and let it sail over you. Have your head tilted toward your opponent to keep an eye on his attacks. Good luck.

Dodging with Counterattacks
Use the same set up as earlier and make sure you can dodge correctly without getting hit. We will now use counter attacks in the following fashion.

Partner one will perform a left Quexada. Partner two will dodge Esquiva right, then step up using the left leg to the front and kick Ponta Pe right. The kick should be aimed at the head, but depending on your flexibility, you can go for the ribs and build your way up. Be careful with your partner. Although we want to train realistically, we don't want to injure our partner or we will run out of partners. Kick at your own discretion. Many times in our beginner's class we just show the kick to the face without contact, or light contact until they students advance.

Do this 5 times each side. Then switch with your partner. Next, you will do the same attack (Quexada) and then partner two will dodge Esquiva Lateral, then kick Benção. The side that you lean to will be the side that you Benção. The final sequence is same kick (Quexada), partner two dodges Quebrada, then counter-attacks with Pisão. This one is the most smooth because Pisão starts from the Quebrada position.

Do all sides 5 times each, then use Armada as the initial attack, then Meia Lua de Compasso respectively. Those are the most used attacks and counterattacks used in the fundamental Capoeira program.

Weaving Kicks

This part is pretty amazing, even at the fundamental level. This is how we practice our spinning kick control and interacting with another player. The thing about Capoeira groups is that they are frequently doing shows and performances, so they can bring out the dance aspect of it during these performances rather than the fight.

I tell my students, that at demos not to sweep or really kick an opponent, but rather, work together to dance Capoeira together. Nobody wants to see that at a public performance. In the academy is where we train the sweeps, takedowns, head strikes, etc. We'll start with weaving Quexadas.

You will Ginga with your partner, then initiate a Quexada like described earlier. Partner two will dodge Quebrada and initiate a counter Quexada crossing you. To evade a face kick just lean back and initiate another Quexada. This will go on and on, but don't return to Ginga. Just keep on doing Quexadas (left, right, left, right, etc.).

One person will be dodging correctly with back to the kick and the other partner will have to lean back slightly to avoid the crossing Quexada. That's how it goes. Perform about 15 left and 15 right to start with. Once you get your staminas up, you and your partner should be able to perform 50 left and right weaving (total 100).

The Armada and MLC weaving sequence will be a little different. You will Ginga with your partner then initiate an Armada by stepping across with the lead foot. At the same time you deliver the kick the other partner will step across to initiate his/her Armada. The dodge is built into the initiation of the kick. As your kicks swings across, partner two will be rotating his/her torso leaning slightly back and delivers the kick. As you finish and land your Armada you will continue back to Ginga just as the following Armada swings short of you.

The cadence of this exercise will be like this for one partner: 1/2 Ginga, Armada right, 1/2 Ginga, Armada left, 1/2 Ginga, Armada right...etc.

The same cadence and concept of weaving will be used for MLC. Just be careful if you kick first, because the second MLC delivered by your partner will be coming as your head comes up from the low MLC position. Keep your head down until your partner's kick passes, then return to the half Ginga.

With both of these last two partner kick weaving exercises, you can start far away and then as you gain confidence and control, try to move closer and closer to your partner. That's what makes it impressive.

Dodge then Movement
We are going to talk about two main transitions after dodging an attack that aren't counterattacks. Sometimes in the game of Capoeira you don't want to counterattack. Instead you want to move, do a cool move, and express yourself. That's your choice. Capoeira is an improvised game and art. We'll give you some choices to practice, but getting in the Roda (sparring circle) is the best way to learn.

For the first sequence you will dodge an Esquiva right, then transition to a Negativa left by putting all your weight on your right hand and slightly leaning right to pass your extended back leg to the front. From here, it's just a simple Rolé to Base, then back to Ginga. This is called "Esquiva, Negativa, Rolé", or "Esquiva, Troca de Negativa, Rolé".

The second example is similar to the first, but without the the Negativa transition. The first movement described above was a dodge, then followed by a switch in direction of escape. In this next example, you will be escaping the same direction as you dodge. You first Esquiva right, then immediately Rolé to the right to escape.

In the Fundamental program, you will learn to put together simple moves to improvise very fancy looking combinations. It's like legos, the lego its self is very simple, but when put together with other simple pieces can create some absolutely amazing structures.

Chapter 9
Quedas (Takedowns)

You've made it this far. Congratulations! Capoeira, as you know by now, has an immense amount to learn about. That's what makes it such a complete sport, or martial art. Strikes, grappling, acrobatics, dance, music, language, play, strategy, and technique are all mixed together in an awesome family activity. Now let's move on to some takedowns, or Quedas.

Vingativa

This takedown is a hip takedown often used in BJJ self-defense technique. I am happy to report many similarities between the two Brazilian martial arts. With your partner standing with his/her left foot forward and right foot back, stand in front of him/her with exact same body position (right foot back/left foot forward). You will be toe to toe about three inches away. Using your front foot as a pivot, swing your back right foot and body like a door behind you opponent and sneak your bent elbow in front of his/her waistline. Ideally, your right ribcage will be on top of your opponent's left thigh, with your left foot side by side with his/her left foot. Initiate the takedown by pushing your hips forward as in a hip thrust, and using your elbow to nudge your opponent over your right thigh. This will take away your opponent's base and his/her feet will come up from the ground causing him/her to fall, or lose balance. No need to do this hard at first. When learning this technique, concentrate on form, then in time you can add more pressure. There are many ways to get into this Queda, and many different variations. This is a great start.

Rasteira

I love Rasteira. It's a super powerful leg sweep with nice circular movement. Let's learn it. Without a partner this should be practiced first, but I am going go describe it with the actual leg sweep to save time.

Start in Ginga right position and step to the base with your left foot. From there, your right leg sweeps forward and your torso leans back with your left hand touching the ground for more base. Your right arm will be extended all the way back running by your right ear facing away from your opponent. Your hips are extended and pushed forward. Your right toes are curled back creating a hook around your opponent's ankle. Make sure to keep you ankle locked to make a more powerful tripping mechanism. You will now, with your opponent's foot escape with Rolé left all in one movement. Your opponent should fall or lose his/her balance when done correctly.

Although you can do this anytime to your opponent, the best time is exactly when your opponent performs a MLC. Match up your Gingas and as soon as he/she steps forward to perform the kick, you step forward to sweep the leg at the same time. When his/her kicking leg is in the air is the best time to pull the leg out since at this time the base foot is the lightest. Remember, it's not kicking of the opponent's leg, but rather, a hook-and-pull.

Banda
This essentially is a standing Rasteira. This time you will not touch the ground with your back hand. This makes it harder and

more reliable on timing and base. The Rasteira gave you the power of the Rolé to take down your opponent. This time you have to have a good standing base to pull the leg out without changing your position, just your sweeping leg. Good luck. This one took me a long time to get good at, because I'm a small guy, but let me assure you that it is very effective at taking down big people once you get the timing and strong base.

Rasteira de Mão

This a sweep performed with the hands by pulling out your opponent's base leg while they perform a kick. Let's explain it against an MLC. As you Ginga with your partner, he/she steps forward to initiate the MLC. You step forward mirroring his position and dodge Quebrada with your front hand blacking. This time your back hand will grab the opponent's base leg ankle. As the kick passes use your front leg for leverage to push on the back of the opponent's knee as you pull the leg out. Your opponent should fall on his/her bottom as their kick rotates them there. This works on other spinning kicks, but works best against the MLC.

Arrastão

This is essentially a double-leg takedown that you might see in wrestling or BJJ. There are many different styles of a double-legs, but I will explain the fundamental one used in our group. To perform, have your partner stand with right leg back (Ginga left position). You, standing in front of him/her, you will enter with outstretched hands to protect from a potential knee strike attack. Advance with your head at the hip of your opponent's left side, right hand wrapping the left leg right above the knee and the left hand wrapping the opponent's right knee. Make sure you have a wide stance for base and power. Now, while leaning your head towards your opponent causing their torso to move left, as you pull their legs right, meanwhile squeezing their legs together. Be careful not to stick you neck out. They will be looking for a guillotine choke, so once you get better at the take down, you must execute it and not stay too long in the set up position. The opponent's legs will become light and you can set them down in a side control position laying down. Although this move takes move strength than some of the other Capoeira take downs, you don't have to pick up your opponent over your head, just enough to pull their legs out, which is literally only a couple of inches. Keep on practicing.

Negativa de Angola

This is the QDR movement from the earlier chapter, but now used as a foot sweep. Yes, although it looks very harmless and stylish, it works! This time, it's not too important to use one arm on the floor. Actually, I recommend using two arms on the floor in front of you. One in QDR and the other in front of your neck area. Your outstretched leg will now hook behind the opponent's ankle like the Rasteira. Make sure it's tight and just pull the leg towards you. You will be surprised how much power you have from this weird position.

Chapter 10
Music

Without the music in Capoeira it would be Karate, or Jiu-Jitsu, or gymnastics, or something else not Capoeira. It is what dictates how fast or slow you will play. Whether you will fight more, or play more. Through the music, the person leading he Roda will sometimes secretly give you instructions with the song sang. As non-Brazilians, a lot of times we will sing a song in the Roda just to learn it and practice our Portuguese; with no other purpose than that.

At high level events, or formal settings, the words of each song do take on a whole new significance. For now, just learn as many songs as you can, and as many instruments. In the Fundamental program we will just go over the Palma (clapping), the Pandeiro (tambourine), Atabaque (Conga drum), and Agogô bell. The Berimbau is the most important instrument reserved for just the higher level students, instructors and masters.

A Palma

The Brazilian Capoeira way of clapping has more swing than just clapping one every beat. It's a three clap--this is what gives it it's flow. If you want to talk in terms of musicality. Then it is done in a 2/4 as follows.

1	**2**	**3**	**4**
clap, clap, clap		clap, clap, clap	

Where the first two claps are eighth notes and the third is a quarter note. If you don't know what this is, don't worry. I didn't either. Just watch the accompanying video tutorials.

Pandeiro

This is the Capoeira tambourine. In Brazil, they have a tamborim, which is a small tambourine with no symbols, and is played with a stick. That's not what we're talking about. The pandeiro does have symbols and our basic rhythms are plaid as follows.

Cadencia-this goes right with the clapping: one, two, three...one, two, three...one, two, three...etc. You can also add a double note on the first note (sixteenth):

1	2		3	4	
out	in	out	out	in	out *(reg.)*
out-out	in	out	out-out	in	out *(var.)*

"Out" signifies hitting the pandeiro with your thumb near the rim (edge), and in signifies hitting he pandeiro with open palm directly in the middle of the instrument.

Atabaque

The Atabaque is played in a similar to the pandeiro, only with two hands. I like to use the following hand cadence with my hands while playing cadencia on atabaque.

Right	Right	Left	Right
1	2	3	4
Out	Out	In	Out

Make sure while hitting the outside (near the rim of the drum) to let your fingers bounce off the surface of the drum head as to not muffle the sound. We wan the note to ring clear, however, when hitting the center of the drum, you can leave flat your whole palm and fingers. We must differentiate between the two different notes.

Using Cadencia, you can play against just about any Berimbau rhythm: São Bento Grande, Angola, Benguela, Regional, Iuna, Cavalaria, Santa Maria, etc. Watch the tutorial videos to see a demonstration. There are a couple that don't work like Samba de Roda.

Also, you will learn more advanced toques like Ixejá in the intermediate program.

Agogô
This is a Brazilian instrument similar to a cow bell. It has two bells to strike a high and a low, although there are some with several bells on it. In the fundamental program you will learn to toques (rhythms).

Marking (Marcação)-In the this rhythm you will play a single note every beat, usually on the low bell. It's like keeping time, but it is a legitimate rhythm. It adds driving energy and is good with fast tempos.

<u>Cadencia</u>-this follows the clapping, or pandeiro and atabaque if their playing cadencia. Even if the drums are not playing cadencia, the agogô follows the clapping. Usually, the toque is:

| |: tick | tock | tick | :| |
| |: (high) | (low) | (high) | :| |

...but you can reverse them depending on what rhythm is playing on the Berimbau. For example, in our group we play "Tock, tick, tock" for Benguela. It varies for each Capoeira group, so make sure to ask the instructor what rhythm is used.

Songs (Letras)

The music is so important in Brazilian Capoeira that it requires you to learn Portuguese to sing along with the choruses in the roda. This is something truly great as it adds an amazing Brazilian energy to every sparring practice. This is what transforms the introverted to somebody outgoing and full of life. A lot of times someone shy is hesitant about singing out loud these new songs, but what I always tell them is, "If you mess up, nobody will know because it's in another language...so keep practicing and sing loud." This usually does the trick and in no time they are belting out Brazilian amazingness.

If you like to sing, then have at it. Go full steam ahead. Just make sure to pay attention to the pronunciations. Your instructor can help you with that or you can purchase a grammar book. There are also a lot of free resources on the web like podcasts, and youtube tutorials.

I have included here a link to the lyrics of the most common songs our group uses. Although we teach in class 1-2 songs a week, you can run ahead and learn more with the following resource. Vai lá!

Click http://bit.ly/capsongs to access.

Video System and Training Access Code

Make sure to go in to the video training area. That's where the magic happens. The resources in there are invaluable. Here is the access code. You will be prompted for your email address. Upon verification you will gain access. Please do not share with anybody. You paid $297 smackers for this amazing system, so please protect my work. Thanks and God bless.

http://bit.ly/capofun

About the Author

Chris Roel, or O Rei as he's known in the Capoeira community, started training Brazilian Capoeira in 2006 in San Antonio, Texas under Mestrando Advogado. He has since traveled all over the United States training with various Capoeira masters and has owned and operated his own Brazilian martial arts and dance studio in Corpus Christi, Texas.

He credits Capoeira and God for his success in health, life, business, and family life. Chris also started training Brazilian

Jiu-Jitsu in 2014 under Gracie Barra Draculino black belt, Professor Leo Cantu.

His wife, Bombada, and son, Reizinho train and help teach in their studio; and continue to be great role models for the fellow Capoeira students. Chris has not only fulfilled his life dream of becoming a published author, but also a best selling author. He has written two best selling books, so make sure to check those out!

Other Works by Chris Roel

"Ginga and Grow Strong: Improve Your Health, Fitness, and Family Life Through the Art of Brazilian Capoeira"

"Ginga and Roll Strong: 10 Capoeira Exercises to Improve Your BJJ"

"Ginga and Build Confidence: Deflect Bullies with Capoeira Techniques, Philosophy, and Lifestyle"

"O Rei's Capoeira Ground Game System: Absolute Beginner to Intermediate Level"

Coming Soon

"Eat and Ginga Strong: Brazilian Capoeira Diet for Health, Weight Loss, and Longevity"

"The 7 Habits of High Successful Capoeira Students: Take Your Capoeira and Life to the Next Level"

www.gingaandgrowstrong.com

Made in the USA
Middletown, DE
18 May 2018